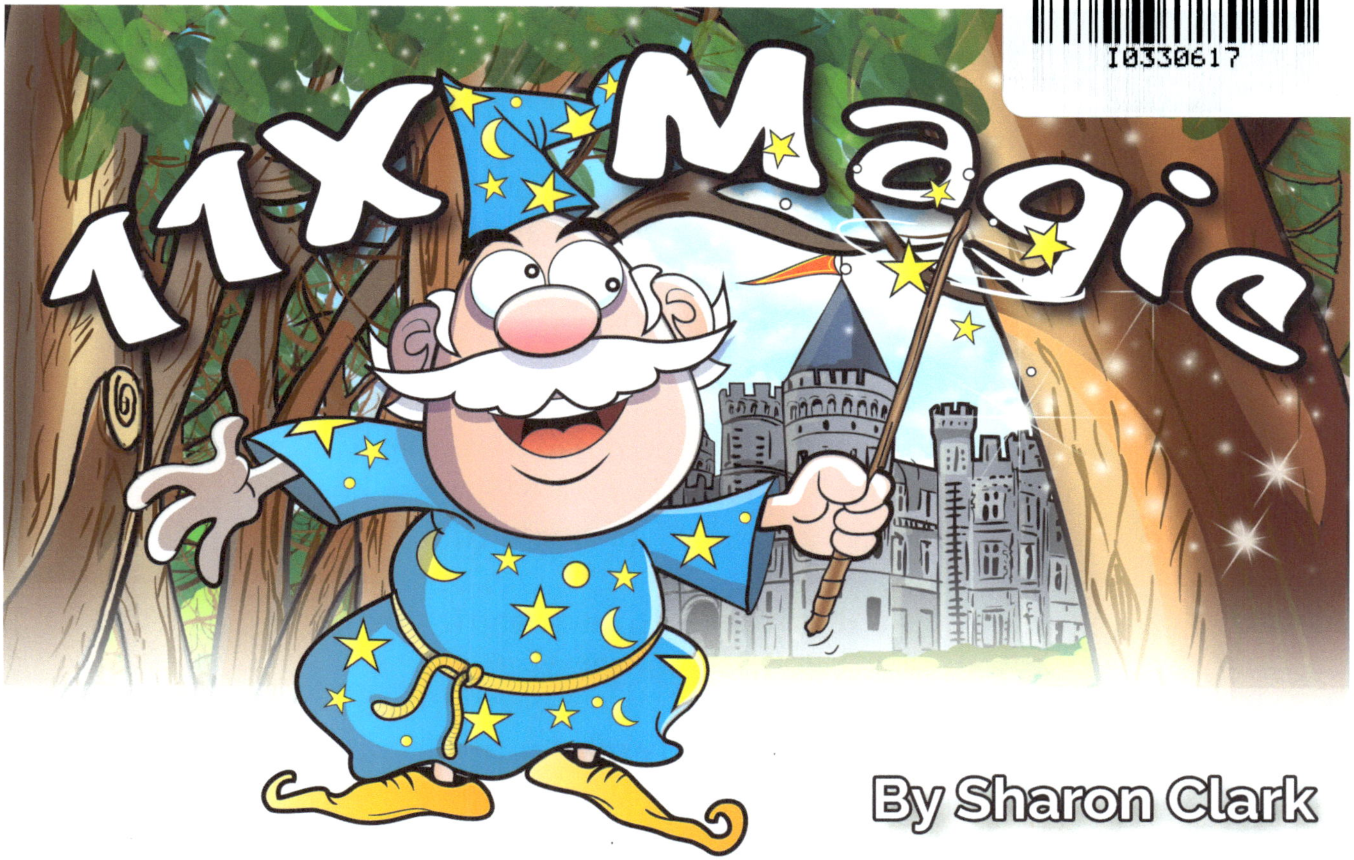

11X Magic

By Sharon Clark
Illustrated by Roberto Gonzalez

DEDICATION

11X Magic is dedicated to Riley Balicki, whose philanthropic activities at his young age are an inspiration to everyone.

His enthusiasm for **9X Fun**, the first book in this series, is an endorsement of the value in making math fun for kids.

DISCLAIMER

In this book, the reader is encouraged to follow the wizard into his castle to discover how magical 11 X math can be.

However, in the world we live in, no child should ever go with a stranger for ANY reason because some people intend to cause a child harm.

The author would like to thank those family members, friends and colleagues who have shown their support for these books in various ways.

In particular, a special thanks goes to Danuta Stack for her unwavering support, encouragement and enthusiasm for the theme of this book and the ones prior:
Making Math and Science Fun for Kids.

A special thanks also goes to the author's brother, Fred Potter, who has shown his support in many ways, but in particular with creating and maintaining a wonderful website for these books:
www.educational-kids-books.com

As always, the author wishes to give heartfelt thanks to
Roberto Gonzalez
roberto@rogolart.com | www.rogolart.com
for his wonderful creativity and expertise in illustrating and formatting this book.

11X Magic

Text copyright © 2017 by Sharon Clark
Illustrations copyright © 2017 by Roberto Gonzalez

All rights reserved. No part of this book may be reproduced in any form or by electronic or mechanical means – except for brief quotations for use in articles or reviews - without permission in writing from the publisher.

For information about permission to reproduce selections from this book, contact
Sharon Clark at sharon.clark@me.com

Printed in the USA

ISBN: 978-0995230378 | Paperback
ISBN: 978-0995230385| Hardcover

Well - hi there!
It's so nice to see you!

How did you find my kingdom here
Where magical patterns in math appear?

You could keep going or come with me
To discover what fun **11 X math** can be

You'll come along and check it out?
You'd like to see what this is about?

How nice! I'm thrilled, so come and see
Just how magical **11 X math** can be!

So here we are on level one
Let's bring it on and have some fun

11 X 1 = 11
11 X 2 = 22
11 X 3 = 33
11 X 4 = 44

You probably see a pattern here
The answers seem so very clear

I bet you already know the rest
Let's put you through your first real test

For **11 X 5** - what do you get?
Do you have the answer yet?

You do! You are so very bright
55 you say? Yes you are right!

When **11** is multiplied by **1** to **9**
Just double that number on the product line

So here they are - the remaining few
I'm sure you know these answers too!

11 X 5 = 55
11 X 6 = 66
11 X 7 = 77
11 X 8 = 88
11 X 9 = 99

Are you ready to learn an easy trick

To find the answers really quick?

Here **11 X math** is also fun
But just not quite as easily done

Multiply a two-digit number for a clue
To a solution that's not too hard to do

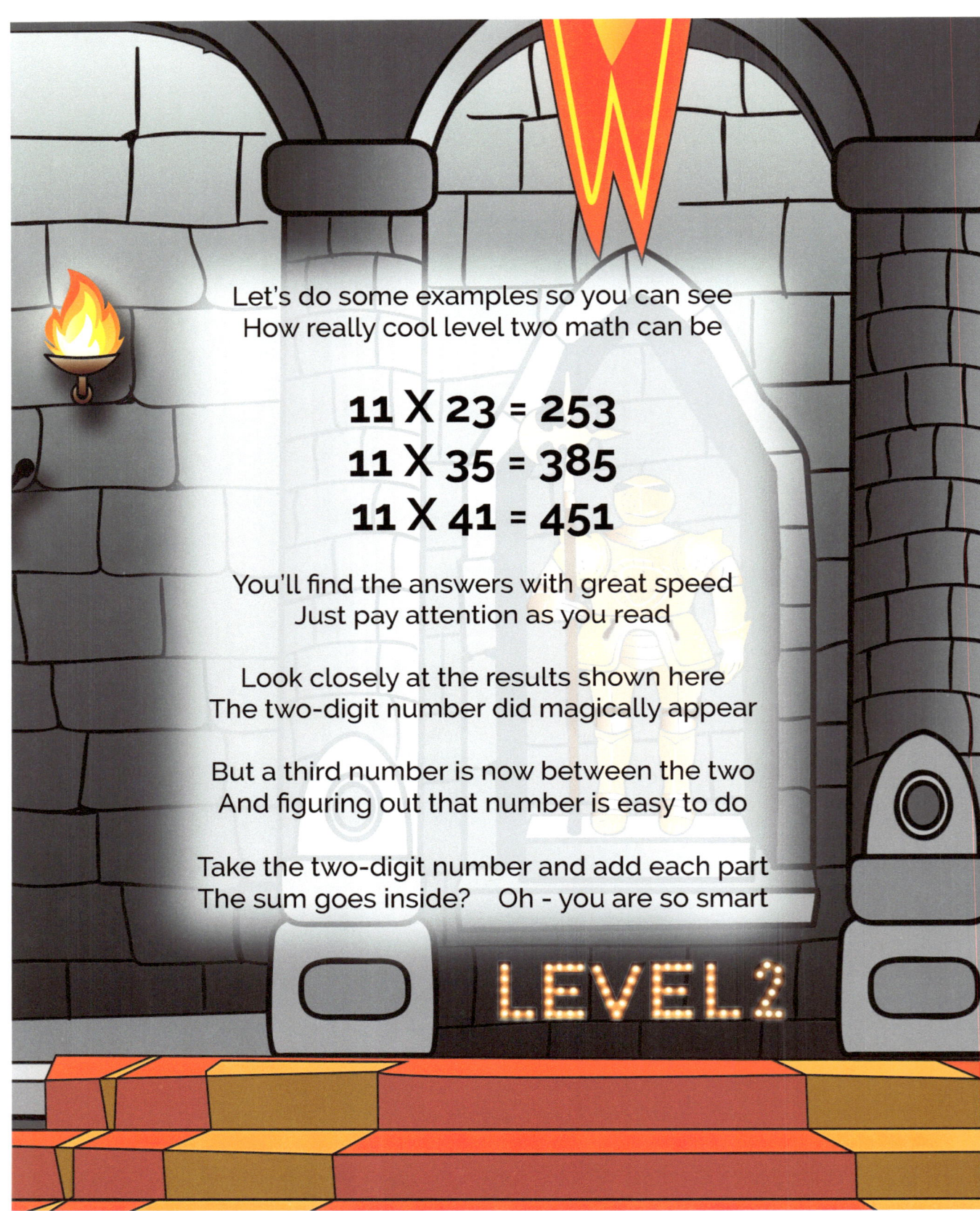

Let's do some examples so you can see
How really cool level two math can be

11 X 23 = 253
11 X 35 = 385
11 X 41 = 451

You'll find the answers with great speed
Just pay attention as you read

Look closely at the results shown here
The two-digit number did magically appear

But a third number is now between the two
And figuring out that number is easy to do

Take the two-digit number and add each part
The sum goes inside?   Oh - you are so smart

LEVEL 2

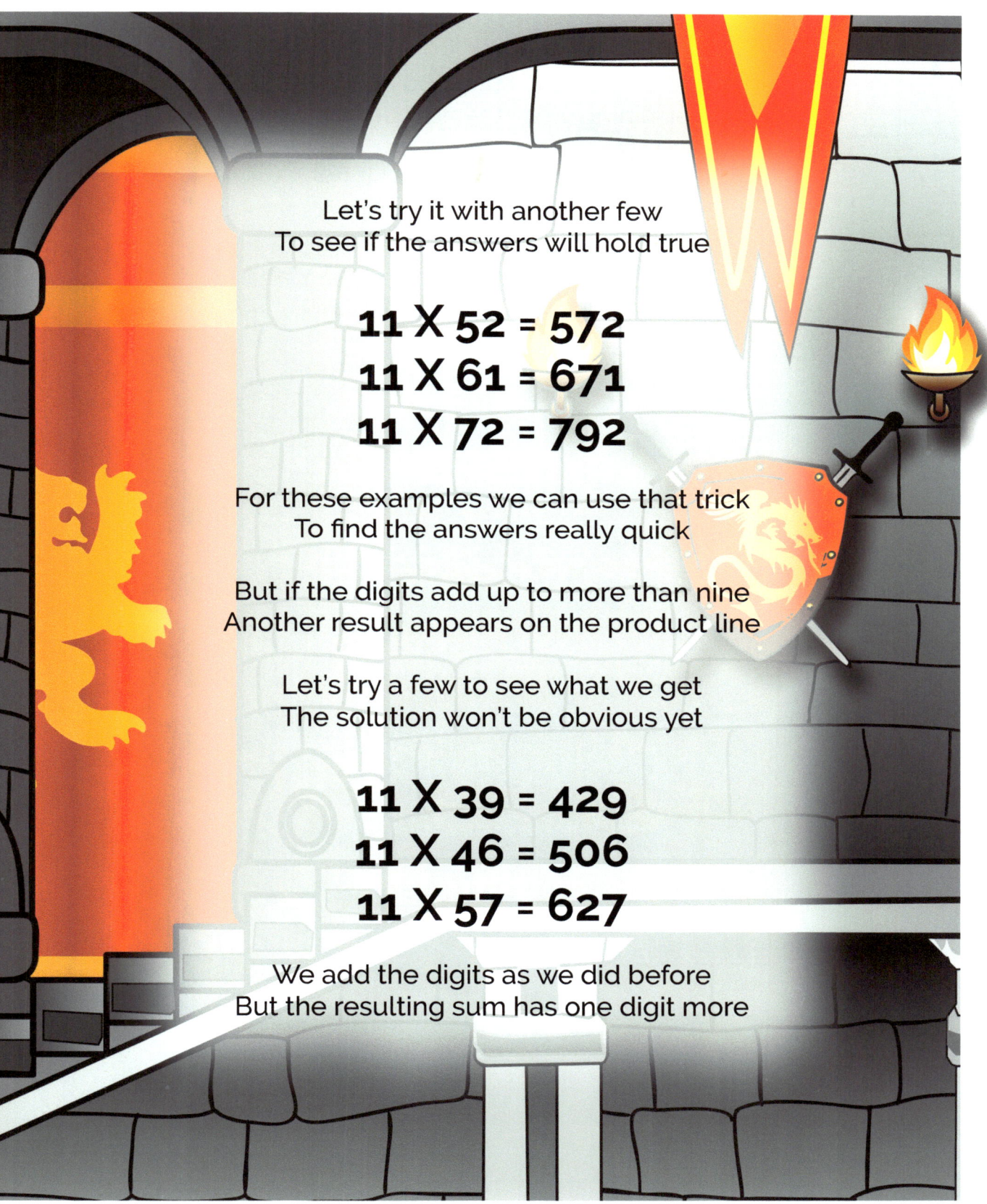

Let's try it with another few
To see if the answers will hold true

11 X 52 = 572
11 X 61 = 671
11 X 72 = 792

For these examples we can use that trick
To find the answers really quick

But if the digits add up to more than nine
Another result appears on the product line

Let's try a few to see what we get
The solution won't be obvious yet

11 X 39 = 429
11 X 46 = 506
11 X 57 = 627

We add the digits as we did before
But the resulting sum has one digit more

The first digit of the summed answer is key
To determining what the final answer will be

Take that digit and add it to
The left-hand digit of the original two

The digit that remains goes in between
The new two-digit number as previously seen

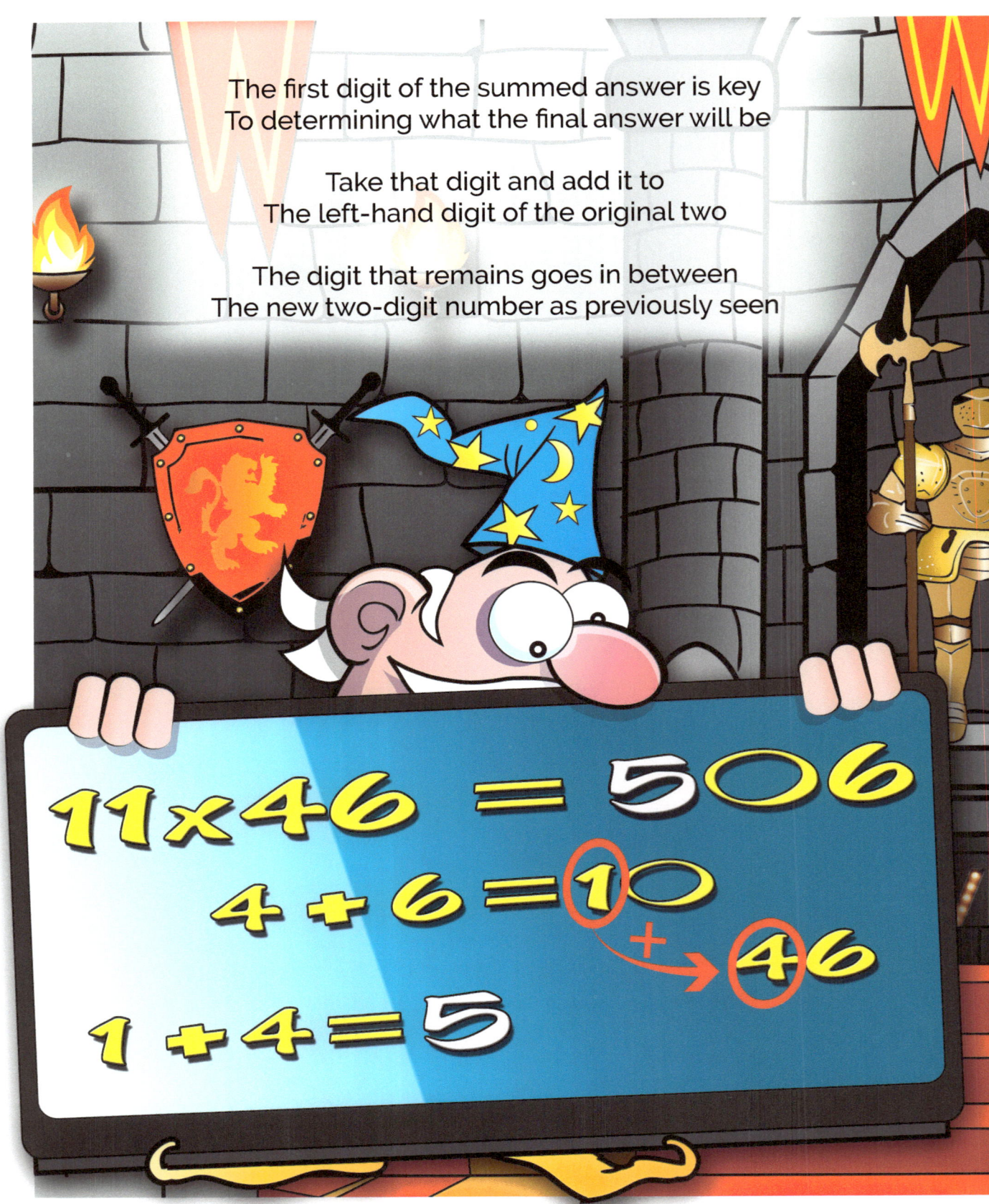

Let's do an example so that it's clear
Watch carefully as the results appear

For **11 X 39** we have a clue
I think you know just what to do

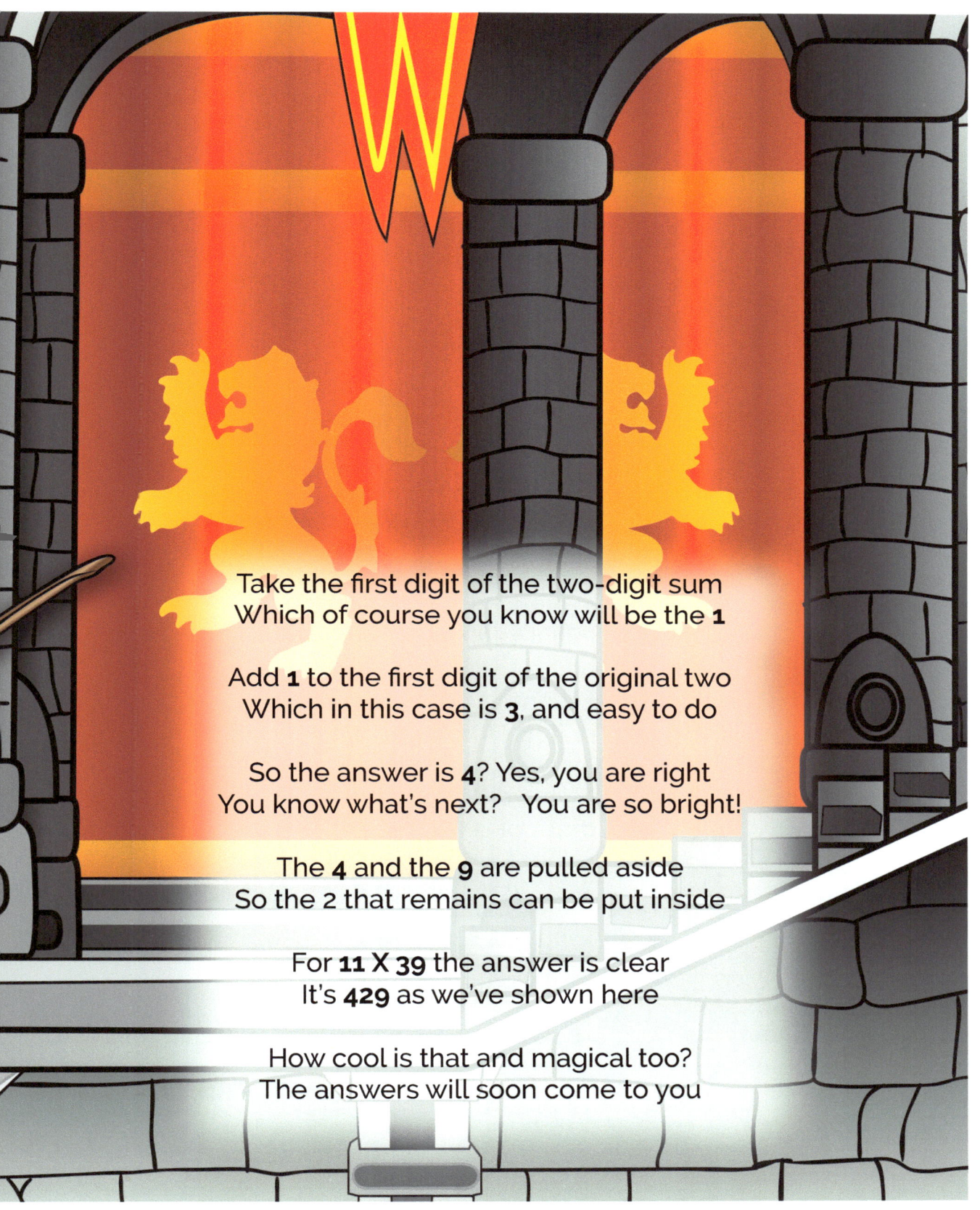

Take the first digit of the two-digit sum
Which of course you know will be the **1**

Add **1** to the first digit of the original two
Which in this case is **3**, and easy to do

So the answer is **4**? Yes, you are right
You know what's next?   You are so bright!

The **4** and the **9** are pulled aside
So the 2 that remains can be put inside

For **11 X 39** the answer is clear
It's **429** as we've shown here

How cool is that and magical too?
The answers will soon come to you

Just practice 'till you are a pro
Then when you're ready, we will go

So, I'll wait here until you see
If you are ready for level three

You're ready now and want to see
How extra magical **11 X math** can be?

The third level is grand but harder still
If you master it as I know you will

You'll be a wizard just like me
For **11 X math** of level three

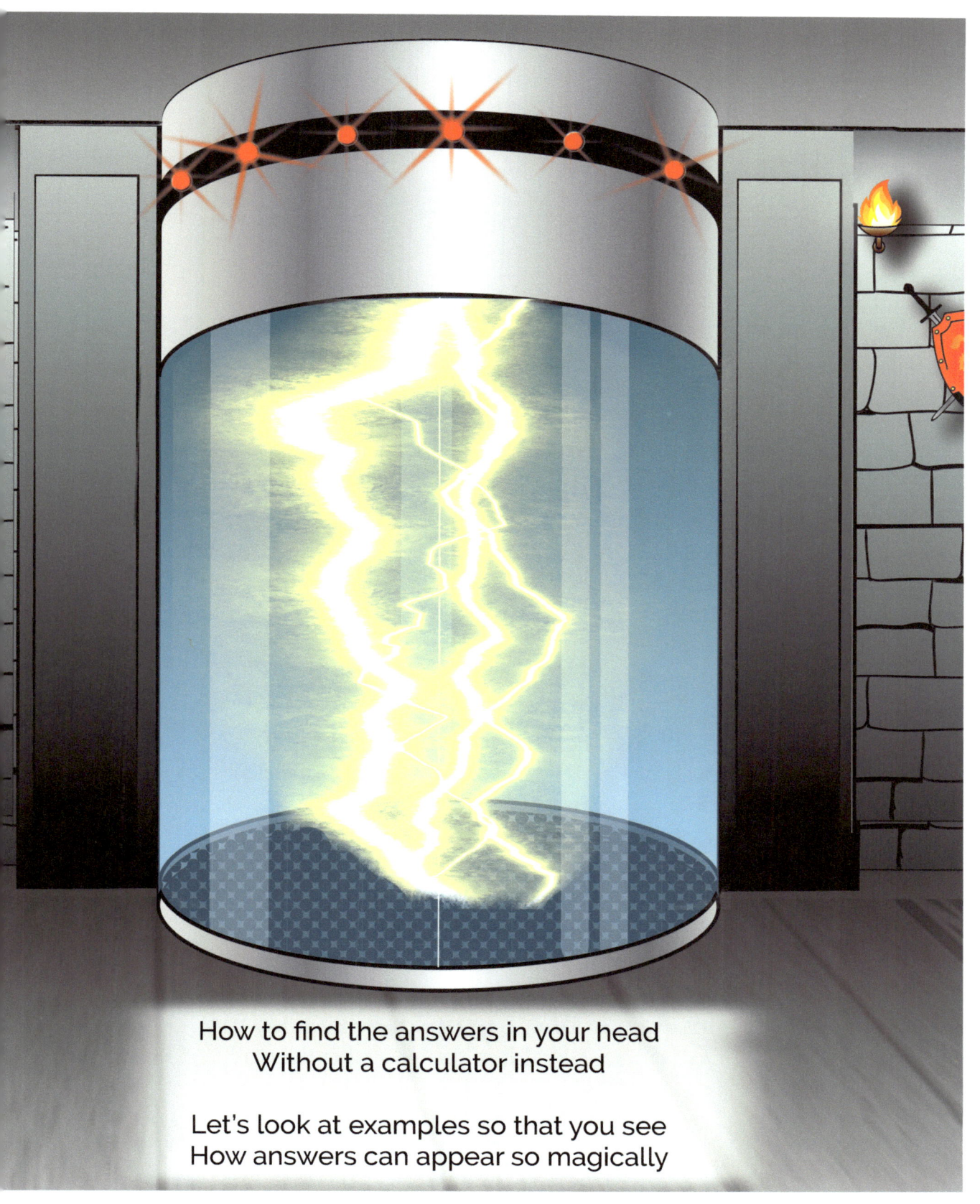

How to find the answers in your head
Without a calculator instead

Let's look at examples so that you see
How answers can appear so magically

11 X 421 = 4631

11 X 545 = 5995

11 X 614 = 6754

Do the answers resemble those on level two?
Do you have an idea of what you should do?

Look closely at the three-digits here
Two of the digits did magically appear

In the final answer at either end
Two numbers are inside. Do you see a trend?

Those inside numbers can be found quickly too
Can you guess what it is that we should do?

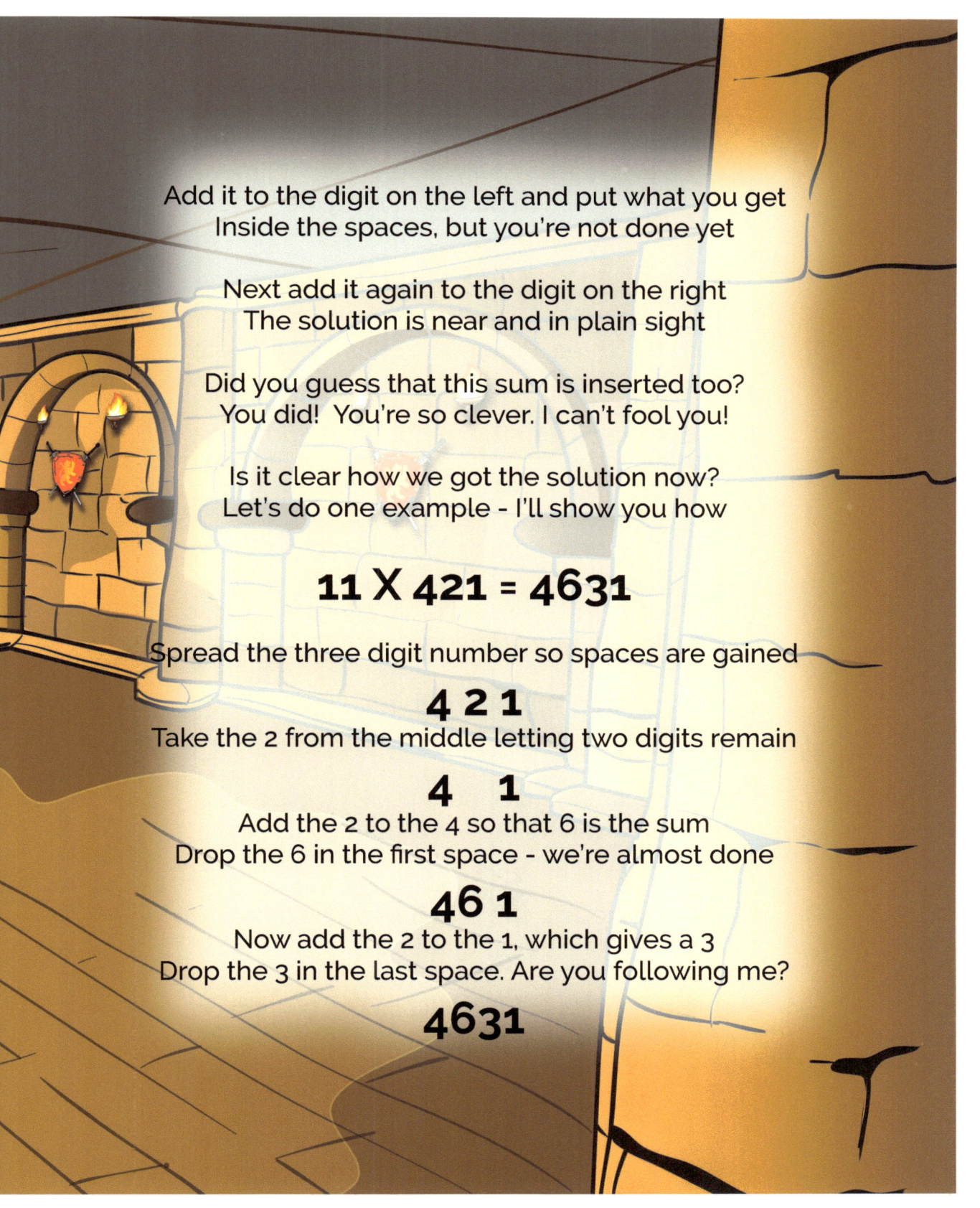

Add it to the digit on the left and put what you get
Inside the spaces, but you're not done yet

Next add it again to the digit on the right
The solution is near and in plain sight

Did you guess that this sum is inserted too?
You did! You're so clever. I can't fool you!

Is it clear how we got the solution now?
Let's do one example - I'll show you how

11 X 421 = 4631

Spread the three digit number so spaces are gained

4 2 1

Take the 2 from the middle letting two digits remain

4   1

Add the 2 to the 4 so that 6 is the sum
Drop the 6 in the first space - we're almost done

46 1

Now add the 2 to the 1, which gives a 3
Drop the 3 in the last space. Are you following me?

4631

There's one more thing to keep in mind
Extra steps are needed if the sum exceeds nine

Let's do an example so you know what I mean
What we're going to do has already been seen

11 X 462 = 5082

Separate the three-digit number as we did before

4 6 2

Take out the 6 from the middle and add it to 4

4   2

When 6 is added to 4 you get
A two-digit number so don't forget

That the sum's left-handed digit will be added to 4
The same way we did it on the level 2 floor

The two-digit number from the sum was 10
Take the 1 on the left and add it to 4 again

Now the first digit of our answer will be a 5
And the 0 will be dropped right by its side

50 2

Finally we add the 6 to the remaining 2
By now I think you might know what to do

Yes, the sum, which is **8**, will fill the last space
And the original **2** will stay right in its place

5082

So now you have seen how to figure this out
You'll get quick with practice, I have no doubt

But one more thing must be mentioned here, too
It's important that you see what you will need to do

If adding the middle digit makes two-digits twice
Then the solution is tricky and not quite as nice

Let's take this example so that you can see
Just how clever and careful you will need to be

11 X 567 = 6237

We'll do the process as we did before
But now we need one addition more

Pay close attention to the steps that you see
And then you will have mastered level three

567
5 7
6 + 5 = 11
61   7
6 + 7 = 13
6237

But the 1 from the 13 now gets added to
The answer's second place digit, making a 2

You've passed this level and soon you'll be
An **11 X wizard** just like me

If you practice, then you'll find
You can do this quickly in your mind

Your friends will wonder and be impressed
They'll think it's magic and won't have guessed

That they can learn to do this too
If you will teach them what to do

So thanks for coming and visiting me
I hope you've seen how magical **11 X** math can be

www.ingramcontent.com/pod-product-compliance
Lightning Source LLC
Chambersburg PA
CBHW041126300426
44113CB00002B/72